# Old LARNE

*by*

## John Hanna

A photograph of the complex railway layout at Larne, taken around 1915 from Inver and looking down over the houses of Jubilee Street, which later became Bank Road. To the right of the large railway shed is the platform for the station, which was then situated at the bottom of Station Road. Pens for cattle were situated close to the market, seen here beside the wagons on the left, and a train turntable was close to the houses. Much of this area is now occupied by the Ledcom industrial estate and the bus station. In the 1940s as many as 41 trains made the return journey to Belfast every day. In 1974 the station was moved further down the line to land reclaimed from the bay.

## FURTHER READING

The books listed below were used by the author during his research. None of them are available from Stenlake Publishing. Those interested in finding out more are advised to contact their local bookshop or reference library.
Robert Anderson and Ian Wilson, *Ships and Quays of Ulster*, 1990.
Doreen Corcoran, *A Tour of East Antrim*, 1990.
Alf McCreary, *A Vintage Port, Larne and its People,* 2000.
Felix McKillop, *A History of Larne*, 2000.

## ACKNOWLEDGEMENTS

The author wishes to thank the following for their help: Joan Morris of the Larne Arts and Cultural Centre; Captain Trevor Wright, Harbour Master, Larne Harbour; Keith Miller, Port Engineer, Larne Harbour; the staff of Larne Library; Mr Frank Pelly, Commissioners of Irish Lights; and Marion Muir, Seaview Hotel. The publishers wish to thank the author for providing the photograph on page 9 (lower) and Des Quail for permission to reproduce the photographs on the front cover, the inside front and back covers, and on pages 1, 4, 7, 10, 13–18, 21, 24–31, 33, 34 (lower), 36, 37, 39, 40, 41 (lower), 42–44, and 46–48.

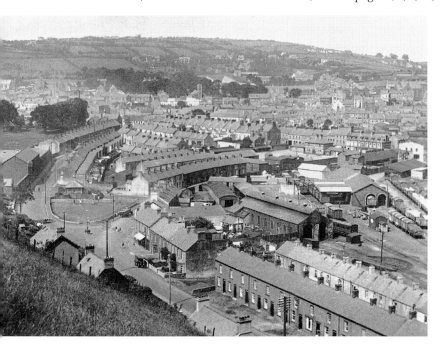

'Old' Larne, as seen from Inver and looking north along Jubilee Street (Bank Road) to the intersection of Glynn Road to the left and Circular Road to the right. Invergordon Terrace is on the left-hand side and just beyond it is Inver Weaving Factory. To the lower right the houses are Jubilee Row, which was built before 1900, while behind them is Queen's Street. While many of the houses remain (apart from those in Queen's Street), this view is now dominated by three tower blocks which were built in 1967.

*Opposite:* In this view the sheds of the coal importers, Rainey and Hall, and Hugh Porter, can be seen on the right, close to the railway yard. Behind the sheds the white pens for holding livestock were also in the railway yard, close to the market which can be seen just left of the centre of the picture. In the foreground is a playground with swings. Behind this, the lodge type building (which possibly belonged to the railway) was demolished when the terraces in Glynn Road and Circular Road were extended to the boundary of the playground in the 1920s. Earlier, New Street, a short street to the left of the picture situated between Glynn Road and Circular Road, was renamed Drummond Street. The houses in this street were later replaced with a modern development known as Drummond Court. The Market House was designed by the well-known architect, Charles Lanyon, in 1864. The area to the right of Circular Road, on the right of the picture, is now the bus station. The chimneys of local industries such as Inver Paper Mills have long since disappeared.

# INTRODUCTION

Larne and its surrounding area is one of the earliest inhabited regions in Ireland. Evidence of early Stone Age hunters was found close to Larne and Glynn. In pre-Christian Ireland, prior to the invasion of Britain by the Romans, the Celtic King of Erin was Hugony the Great. It is said that, as he had 22 sons and three daughters, he divided Ireland into 25 divisions, giving one to each of his children. The area along the Antrim coast, from around Glenarm to the Inver river at Larne, was given to a son, Lathar, and the area became known as the district of Lathar (or 'Latharna' in Gaelic). It is known that a roman galley visited Larne Lough in AD 205 and that there was a settlement in the area at that time. Tradition suggests that St Patrick, credited with establishing Christianity in Ireland, was sold as a slave in a Larne market and later returned to the town on his way back to Britain from Slemish.

Later, between the eighth and eleventh centuries, Larne Lough provided a sheltered harbour for various Scandinavian raiders such as the Vikings. The lough was similar to their fiords and was known as 'Ulfrek's-fiord', from which Olderfleet (the name by which the lough was known during the reign of Elizabeth I) was derived. For their protection the locals built forts and, after centuries of oppression, began to fight back. The end of the Viking presence in Ireland began with their defeat at the hands of the army of Brian Boru in 1014 at Clontarf near Dublin. A later battle is said to have taken place at Larne Lough in 1018.

Larne was also used by Edward Bruce, brother of Robert, to land his Scottish army of 6,000 troops in May, 1315. He was welcomed by the Bissett family of Olderfleet Castle. Edward's objective was for his brother Robert to become King of Ireland; however, after mixed success in a number of battles, he returned to Scotland in 1327. In 1568 Queen Elizabeth I despatched Sir Moses Hill to Ulster to defend the country against further attacks from the Scots. He became Governor of the province and was based in Olderfleet Castle which he had strengthened.

In the early seventeenth century Scottish Presbyterian settlers arrived as part of the Plantation of Ulster. Many became landowners and they came under constant threat from the native Irish. This led to the 1641 Rebellion, during which many atrocities took place.

By the eighteenth century most local people lived barely above the poverty line and there was growing religious intolerance. Conditions were such that many people from the area used Larne as a port to travel to North America. Between 1771 and 1773 over 3,000 emigrants sailed from Larne. Another rebellion began in 1798 when many working class people rose up against the establishment. They consisted of Catholics in the south and mainly Presbyterians in the north, and were known as the United Irishmen. Their northern campaign began in Larne and there was much fighting in the area.

Conditions had improved by the start of the nineteenth century and with the arrival of the Industrial Revolution a period of expansion and industrialisation followed. In the 1830s a coast road was built northwards from Larne and this led to the growth of tourism in the area. By the end of the century thousands of tourists, mainly from the mill towns of Lancashire and Yorkshire, travelled by sea to Larne and were transported around the Glens of Antrim and as far as the Giant's Causeway. The harbour, having been purchased by James Chaine in 1865, was developed to cope with this increase in trade and a regular ferry service to Stranraer was established.

During the twentieth century the harbour played an important role during the Home Rule crisis in 1914 and also during the two world wars. In 1939 Larne Borough Council was created. The tragic loss of the Larne to Stranraer ferry, the *Princess Victoria*, in 1953 caused much grief in the town. In the intervening years industries have come and gone such as BTH, Pye and STC, but the harbour still remains the main shipping link with Britain.

A busy scene outside Larne Station which was opened in 1862 after the line from Belfast to Carrickfergus, which had been built fourteen years earlier, was extended to the town. The station was at the end of Station Road and the market square was close by. The premises of the general smithy A. Snoddy are marked on maps of the area produced in 1903. From the number of carriages, it is obvious that a large number of passengers were expected. These carriages would have been sent by local hotels to transport their guests. One is marked Crawford's Hotel, while in the centre is a coach drawn by three white horses which could easily carry thirty or more passengers. In 1974 Northern Ireland Railways closed this station and moved to the present Larne Town Station, opposite the junction of Quay Street and Circular Road, to facilitate road improvements.

In 1878 the Belfast & Northern Counties Railway extended their railway line as far as the harbour and four years later built a station close to the disembarkation point of the Royal Mail steamers. A draughty wooden transit shed, 226 feet long and 56 feet wide, it was was designed to accommodate both narrow gauge and broad gauge trains at the same time. In this picture the Stranraer steamer is alongside. From the elevation of the view it would seem that this photograph was taken from inside the Olderfleet Hotel. The area of water in front of the hotel has since been reclaimed and is now hard standing for trailers and vehicles using the ferry.

The Olderfleet Hotel, photographed prior to 1907. It was built in 1878 by James Chaine and others as part of a plan to improve the harbour, and was adjacent to the berthing area of the cross-channel steamers. The architect was S.P. Close of Belfast and the contractor was Alexander McFerran of Bangor. The hotel was used as a Naval headquarters in 1914 and was named HMS *Racer* during the Second World War. Later, it was allowed to fall into ruin and was demolished in January 2004. The site remains vacant, although the building to the rear still stands and is in use as the Olderfleet lounge bar and off-licence.

The ferry slip in Larne Harbour. Queen Elizabeth I is supposed to have granted an enactment giving the Ferris family of Ferris Bay the right to operate a ferry between Larne and the northern tip of Islandmagee and this saved a seventeen-mile road journey. According to legend St Patrick is said to have blessed an early ferry and stated that no-one would ever drown in it, however some have drowned while making the journey such as the five coastguards who were lost while travelling from Larne to Islandmagee. Today an hourly ferry is operated by John McLoughlin, mainly taking workers to and from the Ballylumford Power Station. In 1895 the *Irish Golfer* reported golfers using the ferry for the moderate cost of 1*d*. to play at Larne Golf Club.

Ferris Point lighthouse is situated on a rocky promontory at the north of Islandmagee, opposite Larne Harbour. The first lighthouse opened on the point in 1839, consisting of a number of oil lamps in silvered parabolic reflectors 42 feet above sea level. In 1976 a new concrete tower with the lantern over an 'airport style' watch room replaced the 137-year-old tower which was demolished. At the same time new accommodation was also provided. Ferris Point lighthouse was extinguished in March 1994. The property is still managed by the Commissioners of Irish Lights as there is a small dock for loading and unloading buoys to and from a tender.

The Royal Mail steamer *Princess Maud,* photographed alongside the outer quay which was for cross-channel ferries, while a smaller coastal vessel, possibly a coal boat, is alongside the inner quay. A steam crane was able to traverse the quay and the railway terminus is in the background. Today the port of Larne handles 385,000 freight units annually, as well as 200,000 tourist vehicles and 750,000 passengers.

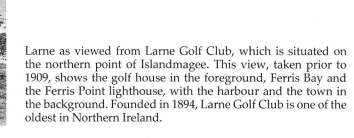

Larne as viewed from Larne Golf Club, which is situated on the northern point of Islandmagee. This view, taken prior to 1909, shows the golf house in the foreground, Ferris Bay and the Ferris Point lighthouse, with the harbour and the town in the background. Founded in 1894, Larne Golf Club is one of the oldest in Northern Ireland.

The opening of the railway line to Larne in 1862 created the opportunity of a steamer route between Larne and Loch Ryan in Scotland. The first steamer on the route was the *Briton*, which made the journey in two and three-quarter hours. Recognising its potential in being so close to Scotland, James Chaine, a prominent local businessman and landowner, purchased the harbour in 1866. In 1871 the Larne & Stranraer Steamship Company was formed, Chaine being a major shareholder, and in 1872 the route was opened by the Prince of Wales, who said that his mother, Queen Victoria, had given permission to use the name 'Princess' on the company's vessels. The early vessels were the *Princess Louise* and the *Princess Beatrice*; however the best known was the *Princess Victoria*, which sank with tragic loss of life in the Irish Sea in 1953. This vessel is the company's earlier turbine steamer, also named *Princess Victoria*.

Passengers arriving by the mail steamer were likely to travel on by rail to other parts of Co. Antrim or to board other local means of transport outside the station on their way to the many hotels in the town. Their luggage was transferred from ships to the far side of the quay by means of this covered conveyor belt.

A Royal Mail steamer docked beside a crane which was on rails and could be moved up and down the quay. Behind the crane the conveyor for the passengers' baggage is extended over the bulwark of the steamer.

Looking east along Main Street, the fine building on the near right was the Northern Bank. The ground floor has since had the stonework removed and now houses a shop while the upper storeys remain intact. To its right was the old Court House which, at the time of the photograph, was a shop which acted as agent for H. & W. Roberts, dyers and cleaners of Bangor. The two buildings to the left of the bank now contain Kell's outfitter's and Apsley's newsagent's and restaurant. This is the oldest shop front in the town and it was at this place that John Wesley preached to the inhabitants of Larne from a first floor window in 1771.

Looking east along Main Street, towards the Laharna Hotel which is the large building in the distance on the left. The extensive King's Arms Hotel is on the near right. At one time Main Street had three large hotels and a number of smaller ones. It was the tourist hub of the town with tours departing to Belfast and all parts of Co. Antrim. To the left is Hugh McKay's chemist shop. Mr McKay was also an optometrist and today his son, James, runs the business. Next to McKay's was the Lindsay Brothers' café, now a branch of Dorothy Perkins.

The King's Arms Hotel opened in 1848 and was sold to Henry McNeill of McNeill's Hotel in 1887. McNeill is recognised as the pioneer of tourism in the area and his legacy lived on for many years after his death in 1904, aged 68. The hotel suffered major damage resulting from a terrorist car bomb in the town in the 1970s. It was rebuilt, but closed for business shortly afterwards. The site was purchased by Dunnes Stores and in 1984 their branch opened in a £2,000,000 redevelopment of the building. Part of the hotel is now also used as a nursing home. The two buildings facing at the far end of the road were on Cross Street, and were demolished in order to create an opening for Upper Main Street. The smaller building on the left with the painted exterior was G. Bonugli's ice cream parlour.

Looking east along Upper Main Street, the imposing McGarel Town Hall stands on the corner of Cross Street. It was begun in 1879 and completed in May 1880 at a cost of £4,000. The funding was provided by Charles McGarel with the condition that the building be used by the townsfolk as a town hall, public news room and library. The three-storey building on the right is currently the First Trust Bank, but originally was the Belfast Savings Bank and was opened by the Right Honourable Sir Thomas Dixon in 1938. Upper Main Street was opened in 1930 to link Main Street with High Street. Originally from Raloo, Charles McGarel (1788–1876) left Larne as a young man to look after family business interests in Demerara. He returned 'with his pockets filled with gold' and became a major benefactor to Larne.

Cross Street and the town hall, looking towards Pound Street. The smart lamp standard probably dates from just after 1891 when Larne became the first town in the province to have electric street lighting. To the right are the Globe clothing shop and a Singer sewing machine stockist. At the head of this street is Pound Street and the attractive building facing the camera was demolished in the late 1960s as part of a road-widening scheme.

Dunluce Street, photographed prior to 1913. At one time, it contained two rows of thatched houses and two of these later became the first two slated houses in the town. It soon became a shopping street. Looking up Dunluce Street, to its intersection with Cross Street, the Halliday Brothers' hardware merchant's and family grocer's shop can be seen. On the left are the premises of Hugh White, draper and clothier, while next door is William Geddis, hardware and house furnisher, and further down Atkins and Company, drapers and milliners. To the right is G. McQuillan, grocer, and a cycle shop which sold BSA bicycles. The buildings on this street remain mostly unchanged.

The Crown Hotel was one of a number of hotels in the town bought by Henry McNeill after McNeill and Co. had been formed in 1896. It was situated at No. 89 Main Street and was a temperance hotel. Recently, it and Magill's shop were occupied by Albert Graham's house furnishers, but the building is vacant at present.

Smiley Cottage Hospital was a gift of Hugh H. Smiley JP, of Drumalis, who provided the site on Victoria Road free of rent and also paid the cost of the building, estimated at £5,000. The foundation stone was laid by Mrs Smiley in September 1901. The builder was James Ferris and the building was completed in 1903. The Smiley Hospital closed in 1988 and after extensive renovation was opened as the Smiley Building, the new headquarters of Larne Borough Council, by the Duchess of Kent in 1994.

Larne adopted the Public Libraries Acts of 1855 and 1894 in 1897. The first Library Committee met in December 1900 and its first library opened in the McGarel Town Hall in 1901. In 1902 the committee appealed to Mr Andrew Carnegie for funding for a free library and received £2,500 with the provision that a site was provided free and that the library would receive at least £125 per year from the rates. The Carnegie Library was built in 1905 on a site at the corner of Thorndale Avenue and Victoria Road. Since the opening of the new town library in 1980, this building has become an arts and heritage centre and it is currently being refurbished.

Larne Grammar School owes its foundation in April 1888 to the beneficence of two of the town's most eminent citizens, Mr Jack Crawford and Sir Edward Coey. Wealthy local businessmen, they donated land and £1,000 each. Originally, it was just a boarding and day school for boys, but it amalgamated with Larne Intermediate School in 1936 and since then it has been co-educational. It had 500 pupils in 1941 and now has 800. This building was demolished and replaced in the 1970s by a large modern school. It is recorded that Sir Edward Coey '... was willing to contribute generously to every project calculated to adorn or benefit his native town.'

Sarah Britten and her pupils at Larne Parochial School, *c*.1910.

*Opposite:* Larne Parochial School was situated on Victoria Road, not far from the Carnegie Library. It would appear to date prior to 1910 and the principal for many years was Mr Andrew Johnston. His assistant in the early days was Miss Britten, who was later joined by Miss Graham. Today the building remains in use as the Larne Elim Church. Prior to this it had been a lecture hall for the 1st Larne Presbyterian Church, which sold it to the Elim Church in 1984. New halls have been attached to the original school building.

The pupils of Larne Parochial School in the playground to the left-hand side of the school building, which is today a car park for the church.

Having opened temporary premises in the King's Arms Hotel in 1930, later in the early 1930s the Bank of Ireland purchased two properties beside the hotel, demolished them, and constructed the attractive art deco building at the far left of the photograph. Although currently vacant, the building still stands. The King's Arms Hotel was one of the many hotels sited in Main Street.

A busy scene outside McNeill's Hotel on Main Street before the days of motorised transport. Many of the passengers on the wagonette would probably have come from the mill towns of Yorkshire and Lancashire, and were most likely bound for the Glens of Antrim. The building shown here is the original hotel which was destroyed by fire in 1909. It was replaced by a larger hotel in 1910, when the tariff was 4/- per day or one guinea per week.

*Opposite:* Seen here prior to 1930, the Laharna Hotel was built by William Holden in 1898. It was rebuilt in 1901, following a fire which gutted also Samuel Crawford's spirit grocer next door. Extended in 1913, the hotel provided accommodation for 2,500 visitors per annum, but during the First World War it became a convalescent home for wounded soldiers and performed the same role during the Second World War. In 1966 the Northern Counties Hotel Chain (UTA), which owned the hotel from the late 1940s, sold it to the Grand Metropolitan Hotel Group who in turn sold it to the Hastings Group in 1971. It was a sad day for the town when the building was demolished in 1999. While there are plans for this site, it is currently vacant. In 1975 the war memorial was moved to improve traffic flow. It now stands in a garden of remembrance in Inver.

MAXWELL'S NORTH OF IRELAND TOURING PARTY.
Starting from Loughview Hotel, Larne, on the 120 miles Motor
Drive along the Delightful Antrim Coast Scenery, a Picture all the
to the World-renowned Giant's Causeway. August 1928.

Mrs I. Maxwell was the 'resident proprietress' of the Loughview Hotel on Curran Road for many years and, even as late as 1937, she was advertising whist drives organised by the hotel. This was an open-air whist drive, held on 4 June 1918. A few naval uniforms are obvious; the hotel was quite close to the Olderfleet Hotel which was a navy headquarters during the First World War.

*Opposite:* Maxwell's North of Ireland tours outside the Loughview Hotel on Curran Road. This hotel was demolished in the 1990s and replaced by a modern apartment block called Loughview Court. The terrace next to the hotel remains. At the time of the tours, the hotel's proprietor was Mrs Isabella Maxwell. The open-top coaches are Associated Daimlers and the tours were managed by J. Gaston, Belfast.

Looking west along Barnhill towards the junction with Main Street and Glenarm Road, the Electric Theatre is the half-timbered building on the left. After 1914 it became the Electric Picture House, and in 1937 the Directors of Irish Electric Palaces Ltd had the building reconstructed and renamed as the Regal Cinema as it was the year of the coronation of King George VI. To the right the four-storey building is the Laharna Hotel which was rebuilt on this site in 1902 and to its left is Crawford's Hotel, Laharna House. The period just prior to the First World War was the boom period for the Laharna Hotel, with 2,500 guests staying annually. It was demolished in 1999 and the site is still vacant and awaiting development. The rear of Larne Methodist Church is on the near right.

Prince's Gardens is a short street extending from Glenarm Road to Victoria Road. At the time this photograph was taken there were no houses on the right-hand side; instead there was an attractive walled garden. While remnants of the garden remain at the bottom of the road, houses now extend the full length of the street on both sides. On the left is the rear of St MacNissi's Roman Catholic Church. The house at the left end of the terrace is The Oratory. Bishop Pat Buckley, who was appointed a Roman Catholic curate to Larne in 1984, and who began to preach independently of the Church from 1986, has a small chapel in the house which is open to persons of all denominations to use.

Housing development began on Clonlee in 1876 with the building of a house for Mr Peter McGregor, manager of Larne Gas Co. Ltd. Many more houses were added before the turn of the century; the second house has a tablet stating that it was built in 1885. The appearance of these houses has changed very little. Clonlee is situated just past the intersection of Prince's Gardens and Glenarm Road on the way north to the Antrim Coast Road.

Curran Road, photographed from the intersection of Main Street and Circular Road. On the right-hand corner the tobacconist and post office has been replaced by private residences, while the Electric Theatre has been rebuilt and is now the Regal Cinema. The railings on the left belong to Larne Methodist Church which is still in use, while the Union flag farther down the road is flying on Victoria Orange Hall, as it still does today.

*4-17-04 We have a very fine view of Larne Harbour from our windows This is a real photo. Edith of the Terrace.*

Bona Vista and Dromalis are the names of two of the houses on Curran Road, which leads to the harbour (Dromalis is probably named after a Friary which was founded nearby in 1180). The tall chimney on the right belongs to the British Aluminium Company which began its operations in 1895, but closed in 1947.

Sea View and Waverley House are situated at No. 156 Curran Road, on the corner with Bay Road and just a short distance from the harbour. At the time it was named there were no houses opposite it and the rooms would have had a view of the lough. Sea View was built as a hotel in 1866 on land purchased from James Chaine. The proprietor in 1938 was A. Charlton. It has always been a hotel and the current owner is Marion Muir. The comfortable sitting room still has the very detailed cornice which was fitted at the time of building and much of the original etched and stained glass is still in place. At one time the lower floor to the left of the door was Gilmour's grocery shop. Unfortunately, Waverley House is vacant at present and is rather neglected.

A view from the intersection of Bay Road and what is now called Chaine Memorial Road (it was originally known as Chaine Memorial Avenue from North Wharf to Sandy Bay) which leads to the promenade. These buildings are still very much the same as they were at the time of the photograph. The tallest building in the row is now the Beach Vista, a bed and breakfast establishment. In recent years two memorials have been erected on the grass to the right: the *Princess Victoria* monument, in memory of the tragic loss of 173 lives lost when the vessel foundered in the Irish Sea in January 1953, and another monument to the vessel *Clyde Valley*, which played a part in gun-running into Larne in April 1914. The Ulster Volunteer Force had been formed as a militia in 1913 to resist the Home Rule Bill for Ireland and to effect a military takeover should the bill become law. The Larne Battalion consisted of at least 450 men. Like others, they required weapons and these were purchased in Europe. Within six hours the *Clyde Valley* discharged 40,000 rifles and three and a half million rounds of ammunition, and 570 vehicles then transported the cargo to towns throughout the province.

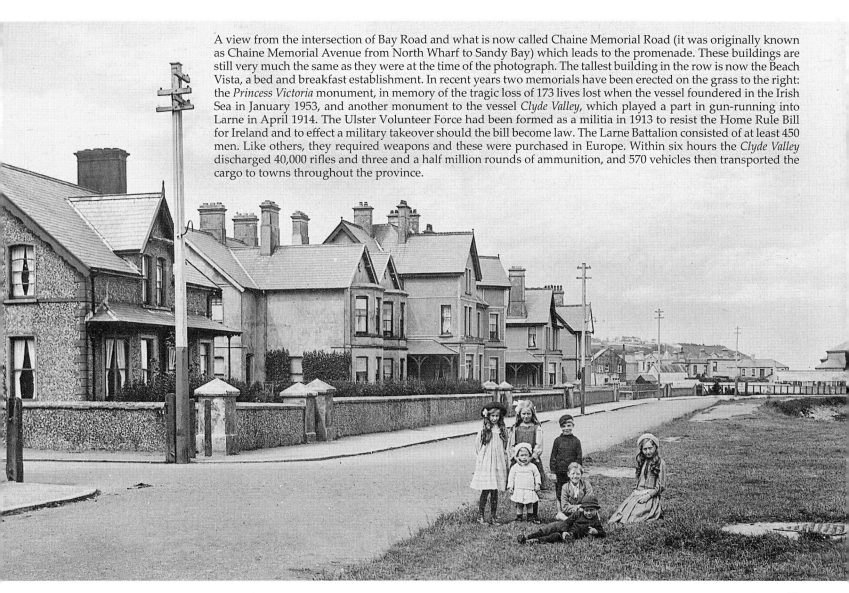

A view, taken prior to 1904, from outside 57 Chaine Memorial Road close to its junction with Bay Road. The Chaine Memorial Tower, which is a replica of a traditional round tower, was built of Annalong granite in 1887 and is 95 feet high. It was erected in honour of James Chaine, a local MP and benefactor, who died in 1885 at the early age of 44. His lasting contribution was the early development of Larne Harbour, and a light at the top of the tower still guides ships into the harbour. The shape of the road is now more curved, passing to the right of the large house at the end. This is Sandy Bay House and has recently been converted into apartments.

To the north along the promenade are the Banks, or Bank Heads, which were a popular spot for bathers. There were separate ladies' and gentlemen's bathing boxes, set some distance apart. This is the ladies' stage; the men's can be seen nearer the town, as can the Chaine Memorial Tower and Ferris Point Lighthouse. A tourist booklet described the stages as 'commodious . . . with ample dressing accommodation, deep and clean water, freedom from currents, and a moderate temperature.' Little evidence of the stages remain and proposals have been made to create a marina on this site, while others are keen it should retain its original natural feel. The modern promenade is raised higher than the old coastal pathway seen here and provides better prevention of coastal erosion. A seam of coal was once found in this area but was not considered a viable proposition.

The path out past the Bank Heads was known as the Cliff Promenade and is still a route taken by the townsfolk of Larne to the Town Parks, Chaine Memorial Park and as far as the Antrim Coast Road. Just above this point is the burial place of James Chaine, set behind iron railings on the site of an early fort.

Chaine Park was officially opened in July 1929 by William Chaine, and it is the burial place of his father and mother. The two-acre park is situated on high ground between the promenade and Glenarm Road and was designed by the Scottish landscape gardener Maxwell Hart under the supervision of the town surveyor, Mr. J.A. Caskey. Chaine Park was presented and endowed by Sir Thomas and Lady Dixon. The layout remains very much the same today with the shelter remaining at the top of the hill. However, all the iron railings were removed for the production of armaments during the Second World War. Sir Thomas Dixon was born in 1869, the eldest son of the Right Honourable Sir Dan Dixon who was the first lord mayor of Belfast and an MP. Sir Thomas was the first mayor of Larne and a benefactor to the people of the district.

Larne Bowling and Tennis Club, viewed from Hawkinge Avenue. The complete absence of houses along Glenarm Road at the time the photograph was taken allows a view of Drumalis House behind the trees. This was built by Sir Hugh Smiley in 1873 on the site of the original Drumalis Priory. Later, a William Crawford sold it to the Sisters of the Cross and Passion for use as a convent. The building has been beautifully restored and has open days for the public. According to a minute book of the Larne Bowling and Tennis Club, '. . . a meeting was held on the 5th September 1907, and on the 9th November 1908 a General Meeting was held in the Victoria Hall for the purposes of founding a club.' It was founded in 1910. The first president of the bowling club was William Chaine, while the first captain of the tennis club was James L. Joyce in 1911. To the right of the clubhouse an extension was built to match the original style and was opened in 1981 by Mrs Ivor Stinson. The grass courts have since been converted to an all-weather surface.

During the building of the Antrim Coast Road between 1832 and 1834 the Black Cave Tunnel – driven through a cave that had been used by smugglers – was the major engineering task undertaken by William Bald, the civil engineer in charge. Originally from Burntisland in Fife, Scotland, he came to Ireland in 1789. In 1933 the road was widened by two feet and a pathway made on the seaward side. A stone plaque was unveiled in 1979 to commemorate the building of the road by 'the men of the Glynnes', local labourers from the Glens of Antrim.

Black Cave Tunnel Larne Co. Antrim.

The Antrim Coast Road, viewed from a point above the Black Cave Tunnel, as it proceeds north through the village of Drains Bay, just a few miles north of Larne. At this time the road was very narrow, but it has since been widened on the seaward side. Drains Bay is now a very popular residential area and many apartment blocks and houses have been built, changing the character of the village since the time of this photograph. It is hard to believe that after so many years the little timber house in the foreground, No. 70 Coast Road, is still there with minor modifications to increase its size.

*Left:* In 1878 a Mr Stewart Clarke of Paisley, Scotland, purchased 'Seaview', a small house and grounds at Cairndhu, from Robert Agnew, and made many improvements, including the building of a large extension. He named it Cairndhu House. In 1918 Sir Thomas and Lady Dixon purchased the property. Lady Edith Dixon was the daughter of Mr Clarke and it is probably the Dixons who are sitting on the verandah in this photograph. In 1947 the Dixon family donated the house and 162 acres to the Northern Ireland Hospitals Authority and it was opened as a convalescent home in 1950. The home closed down in 1986 and the building was sold to Mr. D.S. Rana, a property developer, with the intention that it would open as a hotel. It is currently vacant, but planning permission to build the hotel has recently been applied for.

This card published by McNeill and Holden's Irish Tours shows Mr E.W. Holden (William) and 'Uncle John' of Henry McNeill Ltd at the rustic bridge beside the Ess-Na-Largh waterfall at Glenariff in the Glens of Antrim. This was a very popular tourist destination for those staying in the many Larne hotels. McNeill's would have taken thousands of tourists there over the years. Originally from the north of England, Holden built the Laharna Hotel on the corner of Main Street, opposite Barnhill. Later, he established the Towers Hotel on Curran Road. He was later employed by Henry McNeill Ltd. There is no record as to who 'Uncle John' is, however it could be either John North or John Heggarty, both of whom were directors of McNeill Ltd.

Brown's Bay is situated on the northern tip of the peninsula of Islandmagee, between Skernaghan Point to the east and Barr's Point to the west. Being just a short ferry ride across Larne Lough from the town, it has always been a popular place for daytrips. In this photograph, the owners of the Brown's Bay Tearooms are awaiting their next customers. The tearooms were on the sea side of the road and Skernaghan Point is behind the building.

Inver, from the Gaelic for 'mouth of the river', was the first settlement in the Larne region. It is situated at the mouth of the Inver River and was once a small village of single-storey houses with thatched roofs, set in the shadow of Inver Priory. There were several small mills there and these were probably based in the cottages on Mill Road. By 1940 the old village had been more or less replaced by a new village of Inver which was built further up the hill and is now a busy residential area.

The entrance to Glynn, as photographed from Glynn Brae prior to 1917. While the shape of the road is still the same, none of these cottages still stand. Life changed for the better for many of the Glynn residents in the late 1950s when their thatched cottages were replaced with modern dwellings. The Glynn River passes through the village to Larne Lough.

Glenoe is a quaint and picturesque village at the head of the Glenoe Valley and was visited by many tourists. One of its attractions was the waterfall beside a small church on the hill above the village. This area was taken over by the National Trust in 1968 and the pathways and steps along the Glynn River have been renovated.

Looking towards Glenoe from the west, a touring car is just leaving the village having passed over the bridge across the Glynn River. One of the village's buildings, until recently Maud's ice cream factory, has a blue plaque commemorating the fact that President Theodore Roosevelt's ancestors originated from the area.